Parts of a Life

Parts of a Life

40 Stories on Youth to Adulthood

Chris Ehrlich

1 Minute Stories

CONTENTS

CONTENTS

CONTENTS

CONTENTS

For Colleen

Elementary School

He's being chased by several boys.
Trying to escape them.

They're on an empty soccer field.
25 elementary school boys.

They just downed their lunch.
To rush to recess.

He's the ball carrier.
Until he gets tackled.

They're not playing a sport.
They're playing a game.

With one objective.
Get the kid with the ball.

There's no rules.
No boundaries.

He runs forward.
Backward.

Sideways.
Around.

In a circle.
Never running away from the group.

Running away is for certain boys.
A runner's only chance is to become prey.

He pushes away boys.
Pushes one off his leg.

He stops.
Shifts.

He ducks.
High steps.

He's beaten a pack.
Another pack steps up.

One pulls his jacket.
To take him down.

He chops their arm away.
Knocks them down for trying.

He senses the group wants a new target.
A new challenge.

He throws to a great ball carrier.
Their style is different.

Quicker.
Bouncier.

More dodging.
More weaving.

He watches.
With admiration.

They're not going down.
He's watched enough.

He jogs toward them.
Tackles them in a struggle.

They throw the ball to a runner.
Everyone gives them a head start.

Some fellow runners chase them.
They run to other fields, along the woods.

The group calls to them.
Come back, they say.

They hear the call.
Return to the field.

They have nowhere to go.
They're smothered by the chasers.

Most don't want the ball.
Most want to be in a pack.

He sees the ball coming at him.
Catches it.

He starts to avoid a pack of boys.
Senses it's someone else's moment.

He throws to a possible runner.
Knows they won't run away.

They run toward the group.
Some boys cheer.

A pack goes after them one at a time.
Out of respect for their fight.

They're thrown down after a flurry.
They pop up smiling.

They create chaos.
Throw the ball high into the air.

A boy jumps to catch it.
The school bell rings.

Their run is over before it starts.
Recess is over.

It's time to get inside.
Time to get to class.

Time to read stories about wild boys.

Soccer

He jogs off a soccer field.
Halftime is starting.

He sits down on the grass.
Joins teammates near the sideline.

They're wearing gold jerseys.
With white numbers on the back.

White shorts.
Long gold socks.

He's in 4th grade.
On a youth soccer team.

A parent passes around the snack.
A large bowl of orange slices.

Another parent passes out the drink.
Silver juice pouches with yellow straws.

He eats his orange slices a while.
Decides he likes oranges.

He's surprised by their freshness.
Amazed by their natural orange flavor.

Some ask for unwanted oranges.
Get a few more.

He examines the flavor of his juice.
Makes sure he doesn't want to trade.

Fruit punch.
The windsurfer pouch.

Some ask for trades.
They sound desperate.

They want a different flavor.
Different package art.

Each pouch contains little juice.
Enough for six large sips.

He doesn't drink many juice pouches.
Enjoys each small sip.

Some compare their shin guards.
Cleats.

Some talk about kids on the other team.
Other snacks they like.

The coach walks between sitting players.
Talks not about snacks.

Watch for number 10, he says.
Keep the ball away from him.

Midfielders, get back on defense.
We need you to race back.

Forwards, stay on your wings.
Look for the ball on your side.

His orange ration is gone.
His juice ration is gone.

His break from being a player is over.
There's a game to play.

Running, kicking.
Until his face is red.

Teammates depend on him.
Parents expect him.

To make passes.
Take shots.

Score goals.

3

Trading Cards

He picks up a rookie card.
A hockey player.

Wayne Gretzky.
"The Great One."

Wearing a blue jersey.
With orange accents.

A 1979 printing.
A top pro prospect.

He's in 6th grade.
At a mall for a trading card show.

Card dealers take over the floor.
Fill tables with cards.

The dealer tells him the price.
Says it's a great price.

He notices it's not in mint condition.
Two slight creases.

Right, the dealer says.
That's why it's a great price.

He doesn't have any hockey cards.
Collects mostly baseball cards.

He says he'll think about it.
Walks around.

He sees tables of sports memorabilia.
He's there for cards.

He sees old baseball rookie cards.
From the '50s to '70s.

He's seen those.
At other shows.

He returns to the table.
Picks up the Gretzky.

You're back, the dealer says.
It's a great card, isn't it.

He's holding cash.
To make a rare buy.

He doesn't want to spend so much.
Not on one card.

He's never played hockey.
Except in gym class.

He walks away.
Unattached.

He sees tables of sports apparel.
He's there for cards.

He sees modern cards.
From the late '80s.

He's seen those.
At other shows.

He returns to the table.
Picks up the Gretzky.

You're in luck, the dealer says.
The card's still here.

He sees the imperfections.
Accepts them.

He hasn't seen another Gretzky.
Hasn't seen many old hockey cards.

He makes his decision.
Not because of what he wants.

Because of a rule.
He keeps telling himself.

You don't pass on a Gretzky rookie.

4

Middle School

He's surrounded by 10 other boys.
They're arguing.

He's standing in the middle.
Where the action is.

They're huddled in a middle school hallway.
Minutes before the first bell rings.

They're trading cards.
From every sport.

The serious traders always have cards.
For when trading breaks out.

He reviews a kid's cards.
They review his.

He wants one of their great cards.
Proposes a trade.

He offers multiple cards.
For the one.

He collects certain hot cards.
Only as trade pawns.

Kids are trying to block the trade.
Talking the kid out of it.

The loudest voice is a worthy foe.
He respects their trading game.

He responds to the group's points.
With counterpoints.

He talks about the players.
Upside.

He talks about statistics.
Facts.

He talks about the market.
Peaking value.

He knows what the kid likes.
Knows they want to be in a big trade.

His best offers are limited.
To traders ready for the floor.

He's traded with this kid before.
Smaller trades.

The kid's been around.
Seen other trades.

The kid negotiates.
Wants to switch a card.

He obliges.
Inserts an alternate.

He closes the deal.
Asks if they want to trade.

The kid thinks about it more.
Talks with their consultants.

He waits.
Quips about groupthink.

He doesn't pressure the kid.
The selling is over.

Yeah, the kid says.
They hand him the card.

He hands the kid several cards.
Good trade, he says.

The first bell rings.
School is starting.

He's already learned what can't be taught.

5

Weightlifting

He opens a heavy black door.
Walks into a weight room.

The room is a small square.
Next to a high school gym.

Filled with old weightlifting equipment.
From over the years.

He's in 10th grade.
Wandering in after school.

He's never lifted weights.
His body is telling him it's time.

There's one person in the room.
They don't look like a student.

A man.
In their early 20s.

They're strong.
Muscular.

Not tall.
A good frame.

They're not like him.
In every outward way.

They have long hair.
Move it often.

Big eyes.
Intense.

Black clothes.
Black work boots.

"Hey," they say.
"You looking to lift?"

"Yeah, I'm going to try some of the weights," he says.
"I've never really used them before."

"You can work in with me if you want," they say.
"I can show you."

They talk with an older voice.
Without reserve.

He asks if they're a senior.
They tell him no.

"I used to go to this school, man," they say.
"I graduated a little while ago. I come in here to lift. They let me use my old key. No one's in here usually. It's usually just me."

They seem to like his arrival.
A possible lifting partner.

"Here, let's do the bench," they say.
"Start with the bar."

They demonstrate where to lie.
Where to place hands on the bar.

They demonstrate a good downward rep.
Upward rep.

He does the bar several times.
They add some weight.

"You play sports, man?" they say.
"I'm guessing you do."

He says yes.
Mentions them.

"Did you play any sports?" he says.
"While you were here."

"No, man," they say.
"Sports weren't my thing. I was into other things,
you could say."

He considers asking what they're up to now.
He doesn't.

There are expectations in the town.
He leaves it for them to say.

They show him more equipment.
How to use it.

They keep talking about weights.
Gym etiquette.

Muscles.
Metabolism.

Kids then.
Kids now.

"All right, man," they say.
"I should get going. I was here a while before you came in."

They put on a black leather jacket.
Leave.

He stands alone in the weight room.
More comfortable.

Taught by someone unexpected.
Someone different.

Someone who knows more.

6

Violin

He's holding his violin.
Sitting in a back row.

Surrounded.
By a string orchestra.

He sits with the 2nd violins.
Balancing the 1st violins.

He's in a high school competition.
At a university.

On stage with his classmates.
In a dark concert hall.

They're performing "Adagio for Strings."
Samuel Barber's 10-minute masterpiece.

Many are talented.
Practiced hard for years.

He's not on their level.
Knows his limitations.

His teacher, conductor.
She expects greatness.

He knows his role.
Play his best.

He must be exact.
Read the music.

Hit every beat.
Every break.

Every note.
Keep up.

He's on the edge of his seat.
Follows his teaching.

He begins.
Slowly moving his bow.

Softness.
Hope.

He climbs higher notes.
Only to fall lower.

Dreams.
Unmet.

He quickens the pace.
Holds the crescendo's passionate climax.

Memories flash.
Disappear.

He raises his bow.
Begins again.

Emptiness.
Fading hope.

He slows for the long ending.
So many more low notes.

A life.
Playing on.

When the song feels over.

7

Football

He's ready to run.
His front foot is on a white goal line.

His 60 varsity football teammates are lined up.
Across the same line.

They're wearing full pads.
Their helmets.

The last part of an over 2-hour practice.
Coaches call it conditioning.

It's 90 degrees.
Early September.

"Go!" a coach yells.
They run 50 yards.

He begins a sprint to be first.
It's not officially a race.

He looks to his sides.
To see who's trying today.

They cross the 50-yard line.
He finishes first.

He plays quarterback on the team.
He's not loud.

Not anyone's coach.
Not anyone's trainer.

He believes a quarterback should finish first.
Or nearly first.

They walk back to the 50-yard line
Line up again.

They wait.
Some players haven't crossed the line.

The coaches give them a break.
90 seconds.

"Go!" a coach yells.
They sprint 50 yards.

They cross the goal line.
He finishes first.

It's clear he's trying.
He's winning by a long distance.

"Go!" a coach yells.
They sprint 50 yards.

He looks to his sides.
A few sporting players join him in the race.

They cross the 50-yard line.
He finishes first.

"Go!" a coach yells.
They sprint 50 yards.

He looks to his sides.
The same few sporting players decide to race.

They cross the goal line.
He finishes first.

He sees the fastest few players awaken.
They approach the line with intent.

They're going to join the race.
They should beat him.

He prepares for a track event.
Ready to sprint as fast as he can.

"Go!" a coach yells.
They sprint 50 yards.

They cross the 50-yard line.
He finishes first.

The few sprinted hard.
Didn't run at 100%.

Many players are barely moving now.
Some have given up.

The coaches will stop soon.
Everyone knows it.

He sees the fastest few players are serious.
Ready to race.

"Go!" a coach yells.
They sprint 50 yards.

They cross the goal line.
He finishes first.

By a yard or two.
He doesn't know how.

He supposes they let up the last 10 yards.
He sprinted 15 yards past the line.

The coaches see the conditioning working.
They send the players again.

"Go!" a coach yells.
He finishes first.

"Go!" a coach yells.
He finishes first.

He's not an endurance runner.
Near collapse.

He's first by an embarrassing gap.
The only one sprinting anymore.

He does this at the end of every practice.
In every form of conditioning.

Laps around the field.
A run through the wooded cross-country course.

No coach ever says a word about it.
No player ever says a word about it.

His team has a quarterback.

8

Wrestling

He gets thrown to a mat.
He's laughing.

His teammate twists him.
Turns him.

They're practicing a move.
His turn is next.

A group of wrestlers recruited him.
Asked him to join the varsity team.

They needed some wrestlers.
In different weight classes.

He retired from basketball.
His winter was open.

He knows one finishing move.
The flow of a match.

Their coach goes over a few basics.
They don't practice matches.

He's raw.
Untrained.

He shakes hands with his opponent.
To start an away match.

He's facing a captain.
Of a school twice their size.

They're 5'10".
169 pounds of muscle.

He's 6'1".
169 pounds of muscle.

They're strong in the lower body.
He's strong in the upper body.

He rushes forward to strike.
To take them down.

He gets low.
Lunges to grab their legs.

They kick their legs back.
Fall on top of him.

His forehead is on the mat.
Back stretched.

He uses every muscle.
To push himself up, run forward.

He throws them off.
They tumble out of the circle.

They lunge for his leg.
He stands too tall.

They take him down.
Holding the leg.

He falls to his stomach.
They hop to his side.

They stick their head into his ribs.
Trying to flip him to his back.

He sees the crowd in the bleachers.
Cheerleaders near the mat.

They're cheering for the captain.
To finish him.

He slides out of the circle.
To escape.

The first round ends.
The second round starts immediately.

He's on his stomach.
His side.

They're on top.
Contorting him.

He defends with no defense.
Against their arsenal of moves.

The punishment is relentless.
The round is endless.

He creates pockets of space.
For a wounded burst.

He breaks free.
Frees his arms.

He pushes their head into the mat.
Gets control for seconds.

He locks in a chokehold.
It's illegal.

The final round starts.
They want to end the match.

They slide low to get one leg.
Get both legs.

They rise from their crouch.
Body slam him into the mat.

He rolls.
Gets to his feet.

He tackles them with anger.
Keeps them inbounds.

He's on top of them.
He runs his move.

They break it.
Use his offense against him.

They get back on top.
He's in trouble.

He fights.
To not give them every limb.

To keep free an arm.
A leg.

The clock is winding down.
Seconds are left.

Fans cheer.
For them to finish him.

They're exact.
Trying to run a last move.

He jams the move.
Holds on as the cheering gets louder.

The referee blows the whistle.
The match is over.

Fans clap.
They rise from the mat.

Walk to the center.
The captain wins on points.

They shake hands.
The referee raises their arm in victory.

He's beaten up.
The loser.

He feels powerful.
Victorious.

He went all three rounds.
The captain couldn't finish him.

They couldn't pin him.

9

Baseball

He's pitching to his teammate.
Throwing all fastballs.

He's pitched since he was a boy.
Throwing only variations of the fastball.

"Your fastball looks pretty good," a coach says.
"Let me ask you something. Do you know the knuckle curve?"

"No," he says.
"I sure don't."

It's varsity practice.
He's practicing to be a starting pitcher.

"Give me the ball," the coach says.
"This is a knuckle curve."

The coach contorts his fingers around the ball.
In exact position for the pitch.

He takes the ball.
Finds the knuckle-curve grip.

"I suppose you don't have a change-up then," the
coach says.
"I'm going to show you a circle change."

The coach places his fingers around the ball.
In exact position for the pitch.

He takes the ball.
Finds the circle-change grip.

"Okay, let's see them," the coach says.
"Throw some. But keep your motion the same as
your fastball."

He throws each pitch.
They work on the first try.

"You got it," the coach says.
"Now rotate all of them."

He throws his new pitches.
Every practice.

He pitches to his teammate.
His good friend.

The best player on the team.
Best hitter on the team.

The friend plays left field.
Plays stand-up catcher to help him.

Tells him when the pitch is good.
Why it might be off.

The head coach walks over.
Watches.

"Let's find a game for you to start," the coach says.
"You're ready."

He starts a game.
It's been a while.

He looks into his glove.
Sets up the batter with a fastball.

He looks into his glove.
Grips a knuckle curve.

The ball spins high toward the batter.
Drops low over the plate.

They swing.
Miss.

He looks into his glove.
Grips the circle change.

The ball floats in a suspended state.
Drops into the dirt.

They swing.
Miss.

He does this all game.
In other games, when he's on.

He can't believe it.
He can't explain it.

It's magic.
It's physics.

It's a coach who taught him two pitches.

10

High School

He's singing Nat King Cole.
He's singing Frank Sinatra.

It's after lunch at high school.
The choir room is full.

It's an open room with white tiles.
Wall-high mirrors.

Several girls he knows begged him.
To join the show choir.

They needed more voices.
For the lower pitches.

Their teacher rises from the piano.
To instruct the boys.

On the song's meter.
On the choreography.

They really need the boys, he says.
Like this, he says.

The teacher returns to the piano.
Plays the harmony.

Some of the girls are blessed with voices.
All the girls are good singers.

A couple of the boys are good.
They enjoy singing.

He likes music.
He had a great time in orchestra.

He walks into the choir room after lunch.
Everyone is happy.

Some kids are watching themselves in the mirror.
Some are practicing dance moves in the mirror.

Some are leaning on the piano.
Singing their difficult lines.

Some skip across the room.
To be with another group.

The choir teacher claps his hands.
The kids turn their attention to him.

The teacher tells them to get their outfits.
For a full dress rehearsal.

They get in their positions.
Repeat the songs multiple times.

They're on stage in the school's auditorium.
They emerge from the curtain for the show.

The boys are wearing tuxedos.
Wearing top hats, holding canes.

The girls are wearing dresses.
Wearing gloves.

Some of his teammates in the audience laugh.
Cheer his last name.

They're teasing.
They're not teasing.

He sings.
He dances.

He can't sing.
He can't dance.

They end in a crescendo.
Holding a pose.

His teammates cheer.
Cheer his last name.

Many students in the audience cheer.
Some are standing.

The cheering's different.
It's personal.

He sees them.
He hears them.

In every sport he's played.
In every position he's played.

They never cheered more.

Bloomfield Township

He turns out of his parent's driveway.
For a short drive.

He passes by other ranch houses.
With large front yards.

He winds to the top of a small hill.
Along a nearby country club's north course.

He reaches the traffic light in front of the
clubhouse.
A stage for professional golf tournaments.

He turns on to a main road.
Passes an athletic club.

Passes a luxury car dealership.
Where a bowling alley once stood.

He parks at the shopping center next door.
His destination is the new bagel shop.

He's there to read a book.
People watch.

He's 8 miles north of Detroit, Michigan.
In the metropolitan auto industry.

He's 20.
The summer before his junior year at college.

He sees people from town.
From his youth.

His neighborhood friend's brother.
Who's playing lacrosse in college.

His old school friend.
Who's back from modeling.

His old card-trading schoolmate.
Who's traveling on jets with the college
newspaper.

He's chapters into "This Side of Paradise" by F.
Scott Fitzgerald.
The acclaimed novel-memoir of a 23-year-old.

He knows he was raised in a sort of paradise.
Known it since he was a boy.

He's striving now.
After striving last summer.

He's working at the county newspaper.
Working for a pro tennis tournament.

He knows working isn't enough.
He's on an unknown path.

He knows he can write.
He must use the art form.

He wants to do something.
He wants to say something.

He vows to one day write his own memoir.

12

Granville

He doesn't have a car at college.
The campus is small.

He's tired after football practice.
He asks his teammate for a ride.

His teammate is also a roommate.
A year older.

The roommate has a pickup.
Nearly two decades old.

He asks how he got the pickup.
It's his dad's old truck.

"Hey, you can use this anytime you need it," the
roommate says.
"Can you drive stick?"

"Yeah, I can," he says.
He just learned how to drive stick.

"All right, you're going to prove it to me," the
roommate says.
"You're driving tomorrow."

"Let's go," the roommate says.
"You're taking me to practice."

He drives the pickup a short distance.
To the athletic center.

"Take it easy on the gears," the roommate says.
"Keep it in first longer."

They have a long fall practice.
It's dark.

He drives from the athletic center.
To the dining hall.

"Man, you need to lay off the gas," the roommate says.
"I don't know. I'm not convinced you can drive this truck yet. You're driving again tomorrow."

"Let's go to practice," the roommate says.
"But go the long way. Into town and back to Mitchell."

He drives down a steep hill to leave campus.
Enters the village.

They're 20 miles east of Columbus, Ohio.
In a Northeast-style westward settlement.

He's tested by the village's many stop signs.
He climbs the hill back into campus.

The day's practice ends.
He manages the gears up to the dining hall.

"All right, I guess you pass," the roommate says.
"I'm pretty sure my truck is going to hate me. But you can drive this whenever you need it."

He asks his roommate to use his pickup.
"I need to get something at the store," he says.

"Yeah, sure," the roommate says.
"Just put some gas in it before you bring it back."

He's struck by the casual agreement.
By the handing over of keys.

By the pickup's age.
By the pickup's red stripes.

By the friendship.

13

Loyalty

He's sitting alone.
In a college cafeteria.

A senior.
Last semester.

The cafeteria is mostly empty.
It's a late dinner.

Students don't normally eat alone.
They coordinate with someone.

Head there as a duo.
As a group.

He didn't.
He went directly to the dining hall.

He sees an old football teammate.
Holding a tray of food.

A junior looking for a table.
With a friend beside them.

He was nice to them when they were a freshman.
He welcomed the new kid from Connecticut.

In practice.
In the locker room.

In the weight room.
In the cafeteria.

They're not close.
Not friends.

Haven't talked in a while.
Haven't seen each other in a while.

Football season is long over.
The junior can gain nothing from him.

They won't run into each other ever again.
It's a college campus.

The junior could sit with their friend.
Some others in the hall.

They walk toward the table.
Their friend following them.

They say thanks for that freshman season.
Without saying anything.

They direct their friend to one side of the booth.
They slide along the booth's other side.

They sit down across from their old teammate.

14

College

He has 6 hours to finish.
His section of a college newspaper.

It's after dinner on Sunday night.
He's sitting in a computer lab.

He finished the draft of his weekly column.
He can re-visit it after midnight.

He walks across the main quad.
To the brick student union.

He takes the stairwell to the top floor.
Opens a heavy door in the hallway.

He finds the newspaper's other editors.
At computers in the bright room.

The political news editor.
The literary editorial editor.

The indie entertainment editor.
He is the sport-playing sports editor.

They're starting their sections.
With the print deadline looming.

The late-night session begins.
Time feels plentiful.

They riff about what they've heard.
What they think.

They each forecast what will go right.
What will go wrong.

There's a standard clock on the wall.
Someone looks up to state the late hour.

They fill the air with energy.
Their initial ascent.

One plays their underground music.
One is stuck on the details.

One shares their latest ideas.
He writes another game article.

Someone exits to get snacks.
A tall soda pop bottle.

Some writers barge in.
Declare to the room their article is in.

Others turn in articles late.
Not at all.

Midnight approaches.
The clock above them seems larger.

Their snacks are depleted.
Their drinks almost gone.

The music playing is darker.
Downbeat.

Someone describes their problem.
They're told it's not a problem.

One gets negative.
One asks for advice.

One is emotional.
He is immersed in design.

They volunteer their status.
How far from submission.

They get to the next day.
The chief editor announces the 2 a.m. cutoff.

Their energy is fading.
They have one more flurry.

No one enters.
No one leaves.

The slouching is over.
Unrelated banter silenced.

They share only play-by-play updates.
What's happening to them.

One submits.
Proclaims a last-minute victory.

One submits.
States the exact time on the clock.

One submits.
Proposes they depart to the donut shop.

He touches up his column.
Submits.

The paper will print.
Be across campus in hours.

They clean up their stations.
Leave the room.

Roughed up by the week's news.
Quieter.

He looks around the empty room.
A newsroom.

He's worked in four pro newsrooms by now.
He's hardened by a new truth.

No newsroom will ever be this intimate again.

15

San Francisco

He sees her standing near a beach.
A classic scarf in her hair.

She's tall.
With long, dark brown hair.

Wearing a long, dark coat.
Dark jeans.

Black sneakers.
With white accents.

They're on Crissy Field Beach.
The Golden Gate Bridge spans behind them.

It's twilight, cool.
They're at a casual bonfire.

She's talking with a couple people.
He notices her presence.

It's easy.
Natural.

She's the first woman he's ever seen.
He must meet her.

He observes her a while.
From afar.

She catches him several times.
He doesn't look away.

She notices him noticing her.
He doesn't conceal his interest.

Her group breaks up a bit.
A loud interlude.

He walks over to her.
By a picnic table on the grass.

He smiles.
Acknowledges he's seen her.

"I love your scarf," he says.
"You don't see scarves like that anymore."

"Oh my gosh, thank you," she says.
"I was out all day with a friend. Haven't done my hair at all. She just wanted to come."

"No, I love it," he says. "I'm glad you came."
"I'm Chris."

She tells him her name.

16

Glendale

His wife wants to host a dinner party.
In their new place.

She's thinking Cuban cuisine.
Inviting neighbors, some family.

They're newlyweds.
Weeks into the union.

They're living in a duplex apartment.
With an orange tree in the front.

They're 3 miles east of Los Angeles, California.
Between two large apartment complexes.

She's thinking of the dinner being outside.
In the narrow side yard.

People coming in, she says.
Coming out.

They need two long tables.
To make one.

She's thinking many candles.
She has a vision.

She consults her sisters on the menu.
The decor.

He listens well.
Offers his opinions.

He knows she cares.
Knows it matters.

He helps.
Encourages.

The guests arrive.
At different times.

They check out the kitchen spread.
The apartment.

They lounge inside.
More people arrive.

It's getting dark.
They find their seats at the table outside.

Candles are burning.
Colors are in their places.

She keeps the night flowing.
A hands-off director.

Couples sit beside each other.
Across from each other.

They talk all along the table.
Talk about the city.

He asks everyone questions.
Keeps the talk going.

Couples share stories about each other.
Laugh at each other.

Some go inside to get something.
Come back outside.

The dinner ends.
The night ends.

Their guests don't leave.
They're not in a rush.

One man is a psychologist.
Tells them they'll be great parents.

They say their goodbyes.
Blow out the candles on the table.

They bring items inside.
Together.

It's dark.
Late.

They pass by each other.
Start to smile.

Not about the dinner.
Not about the guests.

About who they married.

17

Burbank

He needs to get outside.
Out of their four-plex apartment.

His wife likes the idea.
She gets her bag together.

His daughter, 1.5 years, agrees.
His son, 2 months, agrees.

The four descend stairs to the front yard.
Somehow.

They're .5 miles east of Los Angeles, California.
Beside the city's Toluca Lake neighborhood.

They pass a gated movie studio next door.
Building-high movie posters tower over all.

They cross an avenue into the neighborhood.
With a double stroller.

They follow well-planned sidewalks.
The sun finds them through the trees.

Each house is different.
Lush plants overtake front yards.

He tells the kids what they're seeing.
In detail.

Spanish tile roofs.
Palm trees.

Adobe walls.
Ironwork.

Gates.
Balconies.

He points out houses he likes.
Yards he likes.

His wife has her favorites.
They like the same statues.

There is much to appreciate.
Old L.A.

They don't see anyone on the sidewalks.
No one walks in L.A.

They wind through the large neighborhood.
Different paths.

He talks about his plans.
Vision for the family.

She talks about hers.
Movement awaits them.

They discuss official issues.
Move on.

Catch up with each other.
Note personal themes.

They turn toward the main street.
Go into a supermarket.

Everyone gets a treat.
For the route back home.

His daughter is learning.
His son is observing the world.

They walk up main street.
Pass by shops they don't patronize.

They pass a coffee shop.
Kid-less people drinking outside.

Dressed to meet.
To be met.

Tied to the industry.
To the city.

They re-enter the neighborhood.
Near their apartment.

They pass rows of bungalows.
Apartment complexes marking the edge.

The four ascend stairs into their unit.
Somehow.

He's tired.
His wife is tired.

They store the stroller.
Show the kids their zones.

He lies on the couch.
His wife lies on the bed.

They take turns talking with the kids.
While the other relaxes some.

They did it.
Their day is whole.

They went for a walk.

18

Portland

He walks over to his daughter.
Tells her where he'd like to go.

Let's go to the supermarket, he says.
To get a donut for you.

She's 2.
Sunshine.

They're in Portland, Oregon.
In Westmoreland.

It's cold.
A winter morning.

She's wearing one-piece pajamas.
He gathers her winter pieces.

Tells her about them.
Let's put on your jacket, he says.

Let's put on your blue boots.
Pull them over your feet.

Let's wear your fun orange hat.
A furry bucket hat.

Let's take JoJo too.
She wants to come.

He hands her a floppy doll.
A colorful girl clown.

An animated cartoon character.
In a circus town.

An upbeat companion.
Positive.

He helps her climb into her car seat.
Buckles her in.

He secures her furry bucket hat.
Hands her JoJo.

He plays music.
An album with thumping beats.

He asks if she feels the beat.
He bobs some in his seat.

She bobs her head.
Smiles at him.

Look at the houses on our street, he says.
The geese in the park.

Look at the small bridge.
The new neighborhood.

Look at the old college campus.
The architecture of the brick buildings.

She offers sensible replies.
She understands.

Look at the main street, he says.
Where people shop.

Look at the interesting mural on the wall.
What an artist painted.

Look at the supermarket.
The big parking lot.

Let's see what donuts they have.
Maybe they have the fun one.

He holds her hand in the parking lot.
Tells her to hold JoJo.

They have her favorite donut.
The bakery's flourish.

Chocolate icing on top.
With artistic lines of pink icing.

He holds her hand back to the car.
Tells her to hold her donut bag.

He zips JoJo in her pocket.
Wherever she fits.

He helps her climb into her seat.
Secures her furry bucket hat.

He plays music from the album.
Turns up the volume.

Let's head back home, he says.
Savor your special chocolate, pink donut.

She takes a bite.
Looks out the window.

Their outing is half over.
The second half is just getting started.

Aren't we so lucky, he says.
To be together this morning.

To get a donut together.

19

Work

"What do you do?"
He asks her.

She asked him the same question earlier.
He finishes the exchange for her.

She says her current job.
Waits for his reaction.

They're at an afternoon party outside.
Socializing.

Standing.
Similar in age.

"What do you like about it?" he says.
"What don't you like about it?"

She pauses.
Considers her response.

"It's a good job. I enjoy it usually, and I'm pretty good at it," she says.
"But it can be stressful."

He asks what she means.
She explains.

He asks his real question now.
To get to know her.

"What do you like to do when you're not working?" he says.
"When you have time."

"Hmm, I'm always so tired after work," she says.
"In the mornings, I suppose I'm just getting ready for work."

He tries again.
Lightens the air.

"Is there anything you're into?" he says.
"That you like to do?"

"I guess I just like to relax and watch my shows
and movies. I read some," she says.
"Sometimes, when I'm up for it, I go out with
some friends and coworkers."

She hears herself.
Doesn't like the answer.

"Sure," he says.
"It's hard with work sometimes to find the time
and energy for anything else."

"Yeah, right," she says.
"It is hard."

No, she thinks.
It isn't hard.

The next night she's at her place.
Sitting with her routine.

She tells herself a truth.
One she tries to ignore.

Her days are not full.
There are no other parts of her life.

Her real relationships were in another time.
She's occupied by nothing worthy.

She's seeking nothing.
Finding nothing.

She's one-dimensional.
Little else.

By choice.
Or not.

Her days begin with work.
They end with work.

Work is her life.

20

Sherwood

He's getting the kids out of the house.
Out of the rain.

They walk through a dark parking lot.
It's evening.

He opens the door to a department store.
His little kids are 4, 3, 1.

They're 9 miles southwest of Portland, Oregon.
In an old city that looks new.

The playground isn't an option.
The library isn't.

The store is bright.
A sunny effect.

He grabs a shopping cart.
Their in-store vehicle.

The youngest kid is the only passenger.
The other two walk.

He buys a soft pretzel.
To share.

Each is disarmed by their piece.
Open to what's next.

They travel around the store.
Stopping in every department.

He tells them what they see.
In every aisle.

Look at the art supplies, he says.
You can't be wrong in art.

Look at the stationery.
Write anything anytime.

Look at the home decor.
Do you like the design.

One kid asks a question.
One makes a loud request.

The youngest enjoys the ride.
Seeing people.

Look at the toys, he says.
Be grateful you have so many.

Look at the sports equipment.
This is how you hold a football.

Look at the books.
Find one you like.

He scouts for small kid-approved items.
Useful in the home.

A reward for not wanting.
Being a kid.

He adds some grocery items.
They're not loitering.

He describes different foods.
Types of packaging.

He reaches the cashier.
It's a reasonable fee.

The automatic doors open for them.
They re-enter the darkness.

Their field trip is over.

21

Entrepreneurship

He hears about another Wall Street firm.
They're bankrupt.

It's the latest historic collapse.
He knows he'll be affected.

His upstart firm provides a business service.
One that can be cut.

His clients have international customers.
They may escape the national fallout.

Days pass.
Weeks begin to pass.

He gets a call at the office.
It's a client.

"As much as we'd like to, we're not going to extend our contract," the client says.
"It wouldn't be good business for us in this climate. We need to conserve cash. You understand."

He gets an email.
It's a client.

"As of today, we no longer need your services," the client writes.
"This is the last invoice from you we'll be paying."

He calls his contact at the client.
To confirm the reason.

"Oh, they told you that?" the contact says.
"Honestly, orders have dried up here. We're probably going into survival mode. You're just a casualty."

He gets a call at the office.
It's his biggest client.

"We need to end our relationship with you," the
client says.
"We're just trying to keep the lights on right now.
We'll pay your last invoice but then we're done."

He calls a major client of his.
The one most immune to the crisis.

"Actually, I don't think, at this point, we should
keep this going," the client says.
"I'd like you to stop the work you're doing for us."

He gets a call he's expecting.
It's a client.

"We decided not to renew our contract with you,"
the client says.
"We agreed it doesn't make sense for us with
everything going on."

Every client is big.
Every check is critical.

Whatever he built up.
Decimated in a season.

He has nothing to do with the economy.
The Great Recession.

He hangs up the phone.
Dazed in his chair.

He tries to picture his next move.
He heads home to his wife.

He tells her they lost another client.

22

Lake Arrowhead

He walks his son into preschool.
He can.

He's not in a rush.
He has time.

They're 72 miles east of Los Angeles, California.
On a mountain.

What do you like to play with, he says.
Before you start school.

The big wheels, they say.
The red one.

He squeezes them close.
Kisses them on the head.

Go, he says.
Have so much fun.

Talk with all the kids.
Be a good friend.

Be a good classmate.
Ask questions.

They run into the playground.
Jump into an empty big wheel.

His mind is heavy.
Knowing only what isn't.

He stops to see every toy.
Every children's book.

Every piece of art.
Every classroom decoration.

He stops to see his kid playing.
Their mind is aflutter.

Knowing only what is.

23

Brother

An older brother cares about his younger brother.
He goes to his basketball games.
Tells him about his experiences.
Practices football with him in the summer.
Invites him to live at his place in San Francisco.
Goes out with him in the city.
Is the best man in his wedding.
Calls him for no reason.
Wants to see him.
Leaves him supportive voice mails.
Travels a great distance to his new home.
Sends him supportive texts.
Offers him his help.

A younger brother tries to return the favor to his older brother.
He watches him on every play in football games.
Visits him at college.
Tells him he's a great salesperson.
Encourages him to pursue his next field.
Tells him everything he knows for his startup.
Talks with him about running a business.
Praises his financial sense.
Stands beside him at his wedding.
Talks with him for hours about life.
Gives him an assist when he asks for it.
Tells him about his experiences.
Walks with him.

An older sister goes before her younger brother.
She teaches him how to ride a bike.
Takes him to a baseball card show.
Tells him to take care of school.
Drives south for his college graduation.
Is his wife's bridesmaid.
Travels a great distance to his new home.
Welcomes him to stay with her when he moves.
Reaches out to others in his job search.

Helps him find a place in town.
Hosts him for the holidays.
Stops by his office.
Answers when he calls.

A younger brother gets to know his older sister.
He tells her she's a great swimmer.
Asks what she's reading.
Learns about her friends.
Visits her at college.
Asks about the pictures on her apartment fridge.
Tells her she's a great salesperson.
Returns from college for her wedding.
Compliments her new home.
Asks about her full story.
Attends her fundraiser.
Tells her any place is lucky to have her.
Asks how she's really doing.

A sibling shares everything they have.
They say they're glad you called.
They know a hug is coming.

A sibling is there for you.
When you need them.
When you don't.

You're part of each other.

24

East Grand Rapids

He opens a metal door.
Walks into a public library.

His three kids are ahead of him.
They're 8, 7, 5.

They stop at the magazines.
He takes a recent issue.

They travel downstairs.
The children's section.

They're staying.
Not leaving soon.

They're 1 mile east of Grand Rapids, Michigan.
In a city with sidewalks everywhere.

He's their personal librarian.
Wonders what isn't here.

Find a chapter book, he says.
To his daughter, the oldest.

They're a reader.
Versed in titles.

They try one.
Start at the beginning.

Find a non-fiction book, he says.
To his older son.

They consider biographies.
Keep moving about.

Find a picture book, he says.
To his younger son.

They consider the best illustrations.
Keep moving about.

The chess board is open, he says.
There's checkers too.

His boys duel.
Make it sporting.

You can build with the blocks, he says.
His older son digs for certain ones.

Look at the art station, he says.
All the supplies.

His younger son sits to create.
His daughter comes over to join.

Look at all the comics, he says.
His daughter judges the titles.

Bring me the books you like, he says.
Pick some to check out.

He gives them space.
To discover.

He sits in sight.
In the teen section.

Reads a few magazine pages.
Interested in the topic.

They walk over to him.
Declare status updates.

They own the section.
Own the floor.

Look at what I built, his older son says.
A pyramid.

Let's display it with the others, he says.
On the counter.

He helps his daughter decide.
Which books to juggle reading.

He helps his boys finalize selections.
Tells them they're great choices.

They all check out.
More books than they can carry.

Each book a reminder of the visit.
Calling to them at home.

To go back.
Explore.

Find themself in a quiet place.

25

Son

My mom debated my preschool teacher at least
once.
My dad entered our front door with a suit and a
bag of donuts.
I was a child for a long time after that.
I knew I was cared for. Dependent in every way.

Mom gave me rides to soccer practice.
Told me to run fast. Kick the ball well.
Gave me rides to football practice.
Told me football is hard.
Gave me rides to baseball practice.
Asked if I hit the ball. Threw the ball well.

Gave me food afterward.
Gave me dinner.
Gave me clothes to wear.
Gave me bright game jerseys.
Gave me a stocked house.
Gave me views on the neighborhood.
Gave me little trouble when I came in late from
playing.
Gave me refuge after school.

Dad gave me rides to soccer games.
Told me I played well.
Gave me rides to football games.
Told me it was for the experience.
Gave me rides from basketball games.
Told me I played hard.
Gave me rides from baseball games.
Told me I was fine.
Gave me food afterward.
Gave me gear to play.
Gave me little trouble when I came in late from
playing.
Gave me trips to the toy store.
Gave me cereals at breakfast.

Gave me the sports section.
Gave me a ride when I missed the bus.
Gave me calm about school.

Mom kept giving.
Gave me guidance to play violin over bass.
Gave me instruction to conduct myself well.
Gave me play in the summer.
Gave me independence at the swim club.
Gave me confirmation tennis is cool.
Gave me message to stop playing a video game.
Gave me access to other towns.
Gave me picture of companionship.
Gave me sense of doing.
Gave me emotion.
Gave me opinion.
Gave me tales of her career.
Gave me visions of her widowed mother.
Gave me facts on what I have.
Gave me an image of a woman.

Dad kept giving.
Gave me guidance to play football if I wanted to.
Gave me tennis majors on TV.
Gave me no pressure.

Gave me takes on the auto industry.
Gave me conversation.
Gave me chronicle of his missteps.
Gave me candor.
Gave me reality.
Gave me picture of humility.
Gave me visions of his father and mother.
Gave me the ritual of church.
Gave me an image of a man.

The giving felt flowing.
I knew my dependence.
I felt a need to earn the giving.
By being good. By doing. Not loafing.
Perhaps achieving.
I gave them my attention. My interest.
Myself.
I determined this is what I could give as a son.

Mom and I went to eat.
We talked. And talked.
About everything.
Her. Me. Life.
And nothing.
How to get change at a bank.

We went to the mall.
We talked. And talked.
About everything and nothing.
We drove around the area.
We listened to music, news radio.
We went to more practices.
We ran errands afterward.
We hung out. Spent time together.

Dad and I talked after my football games.
He built me up. My biggest fan.
He gave me the confidence to work hard.
We went to lunch on weekends. Dinner
sometimes.
We talked about everything.
Him. Me. Life.
And nothing.
How to tip a server.
We went for drives. Looked at houses.
We talked about everything and nothing.
We listened to news radio, sports games.
We golfed at the driving range.
We played tennis.
We hung out. Spent time together.

There was more giving.

Mom gave me tips on dorm living.
Dad gave 4+ hours driving one way.
For the chance I'd play in a college football game.
Mom gave concern about my apartment in San Francisco.
Dad gave me my own path.
Mom gave me suggestion to take care of my work.
Dad gave me support for each venture I attempted.

They gave me opportunity.

There was giving I don't recall.
Giving I'll never know.
Mom walking me in the park.
Dad commuting to work every day.
Mom moving to suburban Detroit, Michigan.
Dad staying on the straight career road.
Mom navigating life there.
Dad ending on the straight career road.

Being a son to giving parents was easy.
While I was innocent. Unaware.

Until I saw them as individuals.
With their own youth.
Their own dreams.
Their own work.
Their own trials.
Until I saw my role as a son.

I give what I can as an adult son.
I fail.
Semi-regular, long phone calls.
Too few emails.
Royal carpet on their visits.
Give some of the love.
Interest they've given.
Seek advice.
Share.
Be an adult son.

They still give.

The best I can do for them now is learn.
From being a son.
Parent my kids as a son.

Be true.
Try to spend time.
Give what I can.
Without expectation. With love.
My duty. A blessing.

I give the part of me that's a son.
So that they might be a child.
As I once was.

26

Basketball

He asks his team to line up.
On the edge of a basketball court.

12 boys.
5th graders in the city's rec league.

They stand at the line.
To start practice with races.

He didn't want to coach his son.
Wanted them to learn from other dads.

Wanted them to have their own time.
With teammates.

He observed their first coaches.
Saw they weren't into it.

He stands in a gym now.
To coach the basketball he played.

Hustle.
More hustle.

Behind the line, he says.
On 3.

He sends out his first group of 5.
To start a league game.

He mapped every player.
On a paper he carries.

Everyone gets equal time.
Each group is balanced.

Everyone gets their chances.
Every position is open.

Kids who never bring the ball up.
Bring the ball up.

Kids who never battle under the basket.
Battle under the basket.

Some don't like the philosophy.
They tell him in practice.

They mumble about it coming out.
Cheer for your teammates, he says.

The next group walks on the court.
They're a mix of abilities.

They run a couple plays.
Play instead on instinct.

Go to the ball, he says.
Help.

Pass.
Shoot that.

The game is close.
Nearing the end.

The other coach subs in his best players.
As some coaches do.

It's against league rules.
Every coach knows the rule.

He follows his game plan.
Sends in the next group.

It's one of their last games.
Some are running out of chances.

He tells the ball handlers to pass.
To two teammates.

They pass to those players.
In the deciding plays.

The players don't believe it.
They pass back to a ball handler.

Ball handlers find them again.
That's you, he says.

Shoot that, he says.
Shoot that.

They get some shots off.
Both players score.

Their teammates cheer.
Their parents cheer.

It's the one shot they ever make.

27

Startup

There's no software code when he starts.
He doesn't write code.

He looks for a firm to code a prototype.
Can't find one that can do it.

He hires a firm.
They can't finish it.

He accepts a partner who codes more.
They're no longer his partner.

He looks for another firm.
Can't find one that can do it.

He hires another firm.
They add the last pieces.

The code is done.
Ready.

The code is his ideas.
Realized.

The code can transform.
Become a bright web app.

Every design.
He drew.

Every function.
He engineered.

Every component.
He tested.

He launches the app.
There's not enough critical mass.

He's now storing thousands of them.
Lines of code.

They're secure.
In a digital storehouse.

The final code is his.
It can do what other code can't.

Such code is hard to create.
They call it technology.

He knows it's too valuable.
For him to hold.

For the right company.
For the right buyer.

He'll sell the code.

28

Money

A dad and son walk up to a sporting goods store.
The automatic doors open for them.

They don't shop often.
They have one objective.

They see colors all around.
Signs everywhere.

They walk along the T-shirts.
Racks of the latest styles.

The son examines one of them.
"What about this shirt?"

"Yeah, it's cool," the dad says.
"I like it too."

"But we don't need it."
"Not a shirt."

They walk straight to the shoes.
They zero in on the wall display.

"Can I help you find something?" an employee
says.
"Is there a pair you want to try on?"

"Yeah," the son says.
"Can I see these in size 9?"

The dad approaches the wall.
Scans the shoes up close.

This pair isn't the most.
It's not the least.

"These feel good," the son says.
"I like them."

The dad sees the bright shoes on his son.
He sees the old shoes again.

Lying on the floor.
Once new.

They have no color left.
Every part of them is spent.

"Okay, get those," the dad says.
"They look great."

"You need new shoes."

29

Tennis

He hits a serve.
Over 100 miles per hour.

It lands out.
By several feet.

He takes a tennis ball from his pocket.
Hits a serve.

Out.
By several inches.

He walks to his metal basket.
Grabs two more balls.

CHRIS EHRLICH

In the net.
Top of the white tape.

He slows down.
Keeps his weight back.

In.
On the line.

That's not coming back, he thinks.
From most any player.

He replays his self-taught technique.
The serve as a weapon.

He focuses on every movement.
Every body part.

His feet.
Arms.

Weight shift.
Backward.

Racket drop.
Ball toss.

Racket lift.
Toss arm.

Weight shift.
Forward.

Racket swing.
Rise.

He repeats.
Tweaks every part.

Fingers.
Wrists.

Elbows.
Arms.

Feet.
Knees.

Weight.
Timing.

He cares less about the result.
More about the technique.

Make it fluid.
Repeatable.

He tweaks the motion for hours.
A ball-striking meditation.

A test of his body.
His mind.

The motion becomes the exact same.
Each time.

The ball blasts across the court.
In a blink.

In.
On the line.

In.
On the line.

In.
On the line.

He hits a basket of balls.
Nearly every ball lands in.

He hits one out.
Another one out.

Something breaks down.
He can't leave.

He hits three serves in.
In a row.

He's satisfied.
With his effort.

His endurance.
His form.

For today.

30

Excellence

He isn't excellent at anything.
He says to himself.

He is honest.
He finds nothing.

He looks more.
Looks deeper.

It's there.
Within him.

He has a gift from above.
He is good at it.

His gift may not look like one.
May feel common.

He sees his gift.
Accepts it.

His gift gives him potential.
He is good without trying.

He activates his gift.
He tries.

He learns his gift.
Shapes his gift.

He sets a high standard.
Reaches obsession.

He goes again.
And again.

He becomes better than before.
Becomes great.

His greatness may never impress.
May never win.

He may never be the best.
May never be close.

He continues his pursuit.
Reaches his best.

He feels satisfied.
No. He can be better.

He reaches excellence.
Part of him stops seeking.

He makes his gift public.
Spreads love through his gift.

He shares his gift.
Teaches others.

He gives away his gift.

31

Faith

He begins his route to work.
Walks in his neighborhood outside the city.

He heads to his first bus stop.
Stands next to the metal bus sign.

Along a main road.
He waits.

In rain.
In snow.

In heat.
In cold.

With a backpack on his back.
Cars pass by.

Parents driving kids to school.
Teenagers driving to school.

People driving to work.
People driving somewhere.

Cars are the mode.
More pass him.

He boards the bus.
Finds a seat.

Inside it is warm.
It is cool.

He opens his backpack.
Reads a library book.

He hears random conversations.
The engine working.

The bus weaves through downtown.
Some pedestrians are walking.

From their parked cars.
To work.

He's at his next stop.
The central bus station.

He walks across a large cement platform.
Sidesteps other riders from parts unknown.

He sits on a bench.
Waits there.

The driver departs the station.
Toward a main road.

He reads more of his library book.
Settles in some.

The bus nears the city's edge.
His next stop.

He de-boards.
Stands at an intersection.

He walks to work.
The one pedestrian for miles.

He says thanks.
For what he's given.

For the bus.
He is this far.

For the sidewalk.
He's off the street.

For his backpack.
He carries less.

For the rain.
He feels the drops.

For the snow.
He feels the flakes.

For the city.
He knows it.

For the walk.
He is able.

He sees his office building.
Turns into the parking lot.

He dodges cars entering.
Dodges cars leaving.

He reaches the entrance.
Grabs the door handle.

He is at his destination.
One hour later.

Thankful for the morning.

32

Greyhound

He grabs a leash.
Snaps the clip twice for his dog to hear.

She already knows the hour.
She rises from her rest.

"Let's go for our walk," he says.
"Let me put this on, girl."

She stands for him to leash her.
Idle for an instance.

He opens the front door for her.
Holds the storm door for her.

"Okay, let's do this, girl," he says.
"You ready?"

She re-meets the sidewalk.
Knows it's a long walk.

They encounter a person walking near the library.
"Is that a greyhound?" they say. "What a beautiful dog."

They encounter a young kid with their parents.
"Look at that dog," they say. "What kind of dog is that?"

They encounter another dog owner.
"Oh, sorry," they say. "He's just saying hi."

She is reserved.
Cool, whatever the interaction.

Patient with the inquirer.
Pleasant with the audience.

"Everyone loves you," he says.
"You're such a lucky girl."

He continues his brisk walk.
She trots by his side.

They reach a park area.
Lined by a forest.

She wanders off the trail.
He wanders off the trail.

She inspects the leaves.
He inspects the leaves.

She stops at the wild grass.
He stops at the wild grass.

"This grass is nice," he says.
"Isn't it, girl?"

Whatever comes from the sky.
They endure.

She pants in the high heat.
He wipes sweat from his forehead.

She blinks through the rain.
He feels the rain hit his hat.

She squints through the snow.
He gets hit by the snow.

"Come on, girl," he says.
"We're fine. This is good for us."

They make the first turn back home.
Not nearly done.

They walk on the brick sidewalk.
Along main street.

She's interested.
Knows it's a scene.

She's glad to be out.
He's glad to be out.

She's not worried.
He's not worried.

She's focused on walking.
He's focused on walking.

"What do you think, girl?" he says.
"I know. It's pretty cold."

They're nearing the last turn.
One last climb.

"Okay, we're almost home, girl," he says.
"Let's finish."

They enter the crosswalk to their street.
She picks up her pace a step.

He opens the front door for her.
Walks in, unleashes her.

She searches around.
Seeing who's home.

He looks at her.
Looks back outside, satisfied.

She did what she was sent for.
She did what she knows.

She showed him the world.

33

Husband

A husband asks you questions on dates.
At home.
In the car.
On a walk.
You say it depends.

A husband eats sushi with you.
You order every type.
Can't decide your favorite.
Tell him to try this one.
You say you love sushi.

A husband lives in Los Angeles with you.
When it's foreign to him.
When he doesn't see it.
Then he does.
You are the best of L.A.

A husband watches reality television with you.
Talks about reality television.
Knows the entire cast.
Considers the human lessons with you.
You tell him what you're watching.

A husband helps you host family and friends.
Supports your theme.
The decor.
The menu.
Your dinner party.

A husband watches your L.A. Lakers in the NBA
Finals.
Your hometown.
Your history.
Your favorite player.
You as a fan.

A husband encourages you to join the moms club.
When you're in a new state.
New city.
Unsure.
You make great friends.

A husband gets you sushi on your birthday.
At a sushi bar.
The best Japanese restaurant.
The supermarket.
You once more say you love sushi.

A husband drives to a winery with you.
You walk out to the vineyard.
Stand for a while.
Get a glass of wine.
You find a table on the grass.

A husband compliments your haircut.
If it's too short.
Way too short.
Bangs or no bangs.
Your new look.

A husband insists you go on the girls weekend.
No way you're not going.
Tell them you're going.
Get ready.
You pack for the trip.

A husband is the parent beside you.
To carried babies.
Bike-riding tweens.
Independent teenagers.
You raise children with him.

A husband doesn't wake you from a nap.
Sleep longer.
He attends to your spot.
Covers you with a blanket.
You need the rest.

A husband backs your interior design.
You find a piece you like.
Find another piece that works.
Find the final piece.
You make the space yours.

A husband remembers being your groom.
Before God.
Before family.
When he's far from his best.
You are his bride.

A husband listens to your music.
Your favorite musicians.
Favorite songs.
Favorite memories.
You play the song again.

A husband doesn't try to change you.
Offers you a question.
An observation.
A challenge.
Your path is yours.

A husband likes your outfits.
Plain ones.
Fashionable ones.
Formal ones.
You say your style can't be defined.

A husband tries to grow for you.
Recalls your questions.
Your observations.
Your challenges.
You mention a wish to him.

A husband supports whatever you do for work.
Whatever the place.
Whatever the role.
Whatever the function.
You say the state of work is flawed.

A husband talks with you.
When it's hard.
When you don't.
When it helps.
You know he wants to know you.

A husband awaits your holiday decor.
On doors.
On walls.
On furniture.
You are the season.

A husband doesn't say anything to you that can't
be unsaid.
Nothing rude.
Nothing hurtful.
Nothing out of line.
You're in a proper debate.

A husband takes long walks with you.
To spend time with you.
Talk with you.
Slow down with you.
Your hands get cold.

A husband respects you.
Your method.
Your mind.
Your strength.
You're a different equal.

A husband listens to you vent.
Without judging.
Without questions.
Without solving.
You say you're just venting.

A husband thinks you're beautiful.
Your smile.
Your ease.
Your way.
You tie a scarf in your hair.

A husband tells you to meet up with coworkers.
After work.
Have a good time.
Stay out.
You say you won't be too late.

A husband is faithful to you.
To the gift of you.
Knowing you.
Life together.
You're the one.

A husband opens the car door for you.
A loud gesture.
His quiet note to you.
He pulls the handle.
You say nothing.

A husband explores the city with you.
Along a sidewalk.
At a restaurant table for two.
Inside a vintage shop.
You say there's a place you want to try.

A husband is committed to you.
Since you said I do.
In all the days since.
Every tomorrow.
You're part of him.

A husband buys you a tiki bar cocktail.
Elaborate.
Tropical.
Indulgent.
You say you love this tiki bar.

A husband loves you.
With a question.
An open ear.
A poem.
You ask if his poem is done.

Hendersonville

He leaves his home.
Walks down the street.

In a planned neighborhood.
New many years ago.

He passes lakefront houses.
Sees the lake between them.

The lake is empty.
No boat is in sight.

He wants to get closer.
See more.

He's 3 miles northeast of Nashville, Tennessee.
In a city with more plans.

He turns on a gravel trail.
Leading to the lake.

He walks through woods.
On a dirt trail.

Trees meet above.
Conceal the sky.

He walks down a slope.
Steps out of the woods.

He reaches the trail's end.
The lake is waiting.

He sits on a large, flat rock.
The lake's edge.

He sees the water still.
Going nowhere.

Sunrays.
Showing the water's shape.

A boat far away.
Cruising.

A factory on the other side.
Smoke leaving a smokestack.

He stays on the rock.
Watching the picture before him.

He's small.
Seeing only part of the winding water.

He rises.
Climbs a few rocks over.

Holds on to a tree with one hand.
Kneels to stretch his other hand into the lake.

He makes his hand move.
Beneath the water.

Because he can.
Because he couldn't.

A wet ritual.
To greet the lake.

To make the picture real.

Food

His friend's mom gives them orange popsicles.
They're playing outside.

His mom sits across from him at a fast-food
restaurant.
He gets to know her.

His dad takes him to an Italian restaurant.
He gets to know him.

His roommates share all their snacks.
They're friends.

He gets a burrito with his fiancée.
They have San Francisco to explore.

His mother- and father-in-law offer breakfast on
long weekends.
He's part of their family.

His brother buys him dinner.
He sees generosity.

His aunts- and uncles-in-law welcome him to their
special meals.
He's part of an extended family.

He sits across from his little kids at a fast-food
restaurant.
He gets to know them.

His sister- and brother-in-law line their dining
room table with dishes for family parties.
He sees easy hosts.

He gets his kids donuts after church.
They pick their favorites.

His sister and brother-in-law fill their kitchen island with appetizers on holidays.
He feels family.

He sits across from his teenage kids at a fast-food restaurant.
He gets to know them again.

His brother and sister-in-law set fine cheese and crackers on a kitchen table.
They're in town.

His kids invite friends over.
They raid the kitchen cabinets.

His other sister- and brother-in-law light up their grill.
They're neighbors in the same town.

He and his wife host a family dinner.
They're the next generation.

The feast is a three-course meal.
A box of pizza.

The celebration is for a special occasion.
For no reason at all.

They talk about parts of their lives.
Talk about the food.

No one longs for an invitation.
No one is an outsider.

No one is far.
No one is alone.

Not while they're sharing their food.

36

Moments

His children are older.
Almost grown.

Little no more.
Closer to adult than child.

He hears one call his name.
Dad.

He hears a question.
He hears the past instead.

Dad, play with me.
Play this game with me.

Dad, look at this drawing.
Look at this paper from school.

Dad, play catch with me.
Play chess with me.

Dad.
Dad.

He sees moments passed.
The parts where he paused.

The questions are different now.
They still begin with Dad.

He only hears a little child.
Being childish.

There is nothing to consider.
He has his answer.

Yes.
Say yes, he thinks.

Always say yes.

37

Dad

A dad brings you home from the hospital.
You are a miracle.

He feeds you with a bottle.
You're helpless.

He changes your diaper.
You have an endless supply.

He rests with you on the couch.
You're growing.

He feeds you in a high chair.
You have a seat at the table.

He is your shadow.
You're walking.

You are 2.

A dad pushes you in a stroller.
You survey the world around you.

He takes you to a playground.
You make fast friends.

He takes you to the supermarket.
You're stepping out.

He takes you to buy a donut.
You hold his hand in the parking lot.

He takes you to the farmers market downtown.
You see the city.

You are 3.

A dad takes you to the library.
You get videos on kids in foreign cities.

He takes you to Old Town.
You see a suburb's soul.

He watches kid shows with you.
You say which character you like best.

He drops you off at preschool.
Your outfits amuse him.

He takes you to a department store.
You see what society produces.

He speaks of your mother by her name.
You know she is herself.

He takes you to a fast-food restaurant.
You taste Americana.

He takes you to the library in your new town.
You leave with picture books.

He picks you up from preschool.
You're not ready to leave.

You are 5.

A dad walks you to school.
You won't need him soon enough.

He tells you about life.
You learn everywhere.

He tells you to talk with everyone.
You say you do.

He tells you to go out and explore.
You map the neighborhood.

He takes you to the library in your new town.
You leave with chapter books.

He shows you how.
You say you know.

He does the right thing.
You may notice.

He goes to your baseball games.
You laugh with teammates.

He tells you to bike there.
You come back hours later.

He takes you to the trading card shop.
You open your pack in the car.

He goes to your school plays.
You're part of something big.

He coaches your basketball team.
You're there for fun.

He makes sure you remember pajama day.
You're a kid.

He goes to your flag football games.
You are pure.

He tries to make your sleepovers perfect.
You'll only have so many sleepovers.

He's a camp chaperone.
You remember.

You are 10.

A dad tells you about friends.
You find your crew.

He takes you to church.
You stand with him.

He helps coach your tennis team.
You go out for a sport.

He sees you play with every type of kid.
You're a friend to many.

He tests his body.
You begin to test yours.

He hears parents say you're just so great.
You have an open invitation.

He works until the work is done.
You ask if he likes work.

He discusses psychology.
You understand people more.

He tells you to be a good friend.
You practice loyalty.

He goes to your lacrosse games.
You find your sport.

He drives you to a tournament.
You ask him questions.

He invites you to dad time.
You're his child.

You are 14.

A dad trusts you with your friends.
You haven't broken any trust.

He works on his marriage.
You know he's all in.

He talks geopolitics with you.
You know the next move.

He watches your mind grow.
You teach him something.

He goes to your plays.
You're a pro on stage.

He listens to music videos with you.
You turn it up loud.

He goes to your football games.
You run on to the field.

He listens to music you produced.
You say you'll make another song.

He goes to your improv shows.
You give the audience what they came for.

He watches the video you produced.
You say you'll make another video.

He goes to your wrestling meets.
You are fearless.

He watches your body grow.
You beat him in something.

He encourages you to move to New York.
You have dreams.

He watches a television series with you.
You don't watch it without him.

He takes risks for his kids.
You ask why we moved.

You are 18.

A dad gives you what he can.
You have opportunity.

He is true.
You are ready.

He is flawed.
You can learn from him.

He tries to do better than his dad.
You sense what you would do differently.

He tells you he loves you.
You know.

He gives you a long hug.
You walk out the door for the last time.

You are part of him.

38

New York

He walks with his daughter up Fifth Avenue.
Not to shop in Manhattan.

They're walking to Central Park.
In the rain.

She's 19.
Living in Queens.

He's visiting her.
Gray-haired.

He wants to see where she sits in the park.
The exact benches.

She leads the way.
Takes him to the Columbus Circle entrance.

They walk a while.
Reach a path with statues.

One stands out.
The Scottish poet Robert Burns.

Her city maintains a statue of a poet.
She tells him about Burns.

She says she sits near the statue.
On a bench-lined path.

She shows him the benches.
Says it depends which one is open.

He wants to see where else she sits.
There's one other spot she likes.

They walk a while to Bethesda Fountain.
She calls the spot beautiful.

It's not a term she uses.
He asks why it's beautiful to her.

She tells him to look around.
Most people would consider it beautiful.

She points to a secret bench.
He doesn't tell anyone about it.

She finds their way out of the park.
Taking turns from memory.

He doesn't need to see anything else.
He's seen what he came for.

Her place to be with other artists.
To share her fashion.

To write.
To act.

To be the dream.

39

Today

Today is happening.
Today is wide open.
Today is about you.

Close the past.
Close the device.

Make breakfast.
Make cereal.

Lift a weight.
Lift your backpack.

Create art.
Create anything.

Walk your dog.
Walk your neighborhood.

Pause for prayer.
Pause for gratitude.

Meet up with a friend.
Meet up with no one.

Take the bus.
Take the sidewalk.

Go to the park.
Go to the city.

Sit at a bagel shop.
Sit on a bench.

Play tennis.
Play a card game.

Be on the team.
Be in the group.

Show love.
Show a smile.

Visit the library.
Visit your living room.

Look out the window.
Look inward.

Tinker with your idea.
Tinker with your collection.

Tend to your yard.
Tend to your place.

Call your family.
Call out yourself.

Watch the streetlights.
Watch entertainment.

Read a poem.
Read a magazine.

Dream.
Dream how.

Start.
Start again.

Don't tell me about yesterday.
Don't tell me about tomorrow.
Tell me how you lived today.

Don't wonder if it was enough.
If it compares.
If you achieved.

Tell me there was balance.
Tell me it is what you desired.
Tell me every detail.

They are parts of you.
They are feats of will.
They are grand.

They are life.

40

Poetry Doctrine

He writes a poem.
About poetry.

To let it be known.
These are his ideas.

His approach.
His style.

Not on poetry as art.
Not on poetry as understanding.

On poetry technique.
On writing a poem.

The craft.
His craft.

The marks of his writing.
His poetry.

Not an automated output.
From global human inputs.

Not a reproduction.
Of the original.

Not an imitation.
Of a creator.

When you see such a poem.
It is his creation.

His doctrine.
Him.

Enter his doctrine.
Dare to see writing.

He writes unplanned.
Pure.

Writes planned.
A sketch.

Writes a beginning, middle, end.
Follow him.

Writes riddles.
Play a game.

Writes puzzles.
Every piece connected.

Writes no literary clichés.
Pre-built drama.

Writes the commonplace.
The challenge.

Writes a story.
Timeless.

Writes a scene.
Life.

Writes about people together.
The design.

Writes about people alone.
A mirror.

Writes a clear message.
Philosophy.

Writes no feelings.
Keep the mystery.

Writes to evoke feelings.
To feel.

Writes positive lines.
Not enough beauty.

Writes no negative lines.
Enough darkness.

Writes vulnerable lines.
There he is.

Writes true lines.
No lies.

Writes no exaggerated lines.
Real life.

Writes free verse.
No restrictions.

Writes stanzas.
Groupings.

Writes couplets.
1, 2.

Writes 1-6 words a line.
As few as possible.

Writes longer lines.
Dialogue.

Writes no I.
Be anyone.

Writes specifically.
Say what it is.

Writes literally.
Each line has meaning.

Writes no metaphors.
Stay on course.

Writes no similes.
Like nothing else.

Writes no common phrases.
Pre-built lines.

Writes no overused words.
Meaningless.

Writes no big words.
Out of tune.

Writes no pretension.
Remove the mask.

Writes common words.
Is understood.

Writes words he knows.
A duty.

Writes no names.
We're all the same.

Writes no company names.
Not here.

Writes no technology.
Obsolete.

Writes no adverbs.
Less.

Writes a capital letter to start each line.
A new note.

Writes periods.
A clean break.

Writes no compound lines.
Rambling.

Writes no complex lines.
Unclear.

Writes no conjunctions.
Interruptions.

Writes no transitions.
Forced.

Writes basic punctuation.
Coherent.

Writes no commas unless in dialogue.
Stumbling.

Writes quotes around long dialogue.
Cinematic.

Writes no quotes around passing dialogue.
The camera's off.

Writes rhythmic lines.
Music.

Writes lines that break his doctrine.
For the song.

His doctrine is natural.
Born without thought.

Documented now.
Only to document.

Follow your doctrine.
Let it happen first.

Others will chime.
A poet doesn't have a doctrine.

They do.
Find it.

A poet's doctrine is right there.
Written for all to see.

In every poem.
Every line.

Every word.

ACKNOWLEDGMENTS

Thank you to these special people for their support of me and this book: my wife, my kids, my parents, my siblings, and my extended family.

Without you, there are no stories.
With you, there is life.

Chris Ehrlich is an original (human) author, entrepreneur, husband, dad of 3, and tennis hacker. He holds a degree in English and political science from Denison University. He's lived in Michigan, Ohio, California, and Oregon. He writes in Tennessee.